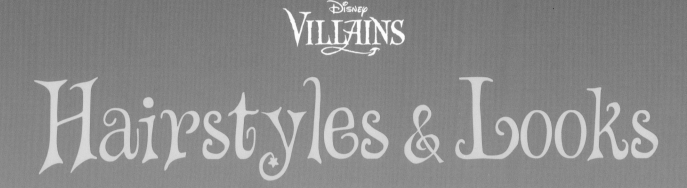

Disney VILLAINS
Hairstyles & Looks

EDDA USA

Disney Villains Hairstyles & Looks

© 2015 Disney Enterprises, Inc.

Author: Harpa Omarsdottir
Photographer: ©Gassi.is
Photoshop on pages 12–13, 22–23, 32–33, 42–43, 52–53, 60–61, 68–69, 78–79, 86–87: Olof Erla Einarsdottir
Costume Designer: Maria Olafsdottir
Makeup artist: Frida Maria Hardardottir
Layout and design: Greta Osp
Cover design: Gassi.is, Olafur Gunnar Gudlaugsson
Editors: Svala Thormodsdottir, svala@edda.is and
Tinna Proppe, tinna@eddausa.com
Printing: Printed in Canada

Distributed by Midpoint Book Sales & Distribution

ISBN: 978-1-94078-721-3

www.eddausa.com

Welcome to the exciting world of the Disney Villains!

On these pages you will find 33 fantastic hairstyles along with some useful tips and tricks to create your own look inspired by nine of the most iconic villains of all times.

Use the book as inspiration and find your own style that represents the various styles of the villains. When creating your look you can do no wrong and the most successful looks are the ones created from anything and everything you can find in your own home.

Some of the styles in this book can even be used for your everyday look while others are a bit more adventurous.

Dive in, be inspired but above all ...

HAVE FUN!

Maleficent

What's the Story?
Maleficent is a forest fairy that has lost her wings and she is very angry when not invited to the christening of baby Aurora who also goes by the name of Sleeping Beauty. She succumbs to her dark thoughts and turns to evil magic when she curses Aurora to a lifelong sleep much to the king's despair. Maleficent can turn into a fierce dragon and has magical powers. She is mysterious, powerful and larger than life.

Color Palette
Maleficent is most often seen wearing black and that is her primary color. She is also seen with dark purple added to her clothing and her skin is sometimes green.

What to Wear
Long elegant black gowns
Big sleeved clothing
Clothing with dragon details

Makeup
Wear dark and heavy smokey eye makeup, purple or dark grey
Dark red lipstick

Accessories
A staff
Wings
Plush crow

Evil Queen

What's the Story?

The Evil Queen is the main villain in the classic fairy-tale about Snow White. She is filled with jealousy of Snow White and will stop at no end to become the fairest of everyone. Enraged by Snow White's beauty she orders her to be killed. She is very intelligent, ruthless and has a regal arrogance to her. She is sometimes portrait as an old witch, which is the shape she is in when she gives Snow White a poisonous apple.

Color Palette

Dark purple and black are the primary colors of the Evil Queen and she is often portrait wearing a golden crown. When in her old witch form she has long white hair and her skin is very white with big grey bags under her eyes and is usually wearing a hooded cape.

What to Wear

A long and regal purple gown or a dress
A black cape
Regal clothing with a high collar

Makeup

She wears dark purple eye shadow and a dark red lipstick. She has very iconic thin and high black eyebrows.

Accessories

A crown
A pendant
An apple
A mirror

Madam Mim

What's the Story?
Madam Mim is Merlin's main rival in the classic adventure *The Sword in the Stone*. She is a very powerful witch who is equal or even more powerful than Merlin himself. She however has a big flaw, which is her overconfidence. She is a specialist in dark magic but her biggest ability is being a shapeshifter and she can turn herself into anything she wants. She is a little evil and mean but above all she is funny, mischievous and a little bit clumsy.

Color Palette
Her main colors are pink and purple. She has iconic purple hair and her clothing is most often pink or purple and occasionally blue.

What to Wear
Pink or purple everyday clothing
Big skirt
A vest

Makeup
Madam Mim does not take part in the frivolous act of putting on makeup. She has iconic dark eyebrows and very rosy cheeks.

Accessories
A broom
A cauldron
A plush cat
Cristal ball

Ursula

What's the Story?
Ursula is everyone's favorite villain from the story about the little mermaid Ariel. She is a powerful sea witch that tricks Ariel into giving up her voice. Ursula's main agenda is to get her hands on Triton's trident so she can rule the ocean. Ursula's form is a cecaelia, a half human and half octopus. She is powerful, manipulative, very charming and funny.

Color Palette
Various colors of blue mixed with black is a good color palette for Ursula as well as purple, seeing as she is most often portrait with purpled color skin.

What to Wear
Black strapless tops
Lace shirt underneath
Blue, black or purple tops with sequins

Makeup
Ursula wears very heavy blue eye shadow that goes up to her forehead. She has very iconic eyebrows high up on her forehead and she wears red lipstick as well as bright red nail polish.

Accessories
Trident
A shell pendant
Anything related to the ocean
Seashell earrings

Captain Hook

What's the Story?
Captain Hook is Peter Pan's nemesis and is very devoted to finding him and killing him. Peter Pan cut off his hand in a sword fight and fed it to the large crocodile that roams the waters in Neverland. Hook is terrified of the crocodile and is extremely bitter about the fact that not only did Peter beat him in a fight but he can not fly like Peter can. Hook is arrogant and loud as well as being funny, childish and cowardly.

Color Palette
Hooks pirate coat is a bright red color and his hat is burgundy. His palette is brighter than some of the other villains with red being his iconic color.

What to Wear
A long coat with buttons
A white shirt with a big pleaded button down
A detailed belt
Clothing with embroidery and detail
Black boots
A hat with a feather
White knee high socks

Makeup
Captain Hook understandably does not wear makeup. To get his iconic look you can use black color to accentuate the eyebrows and use black eyeliner to frame the eyes. If you want to go all out you can draw his iconic mustache on your upper lip.

Accessories
A hook
A fencing sword
Telescope
Compass

Cruella de Vil

What's the Story?
Cruella De Vil is the iconic and fabulous villain in the classic tale *101 Dalmatians*. She is a wealthy heiress who is obsessed with fashion and her main wish is to use the skins of Dalmatian puppies to create her very own fur coat. Cruella will stop at no length to get what she wants but thankfully she has great difficulty getting her hands on the adorable little puppies. She is greedy and selfish as well as being sarcastic, glamorous and very chic.

Color Palette
Cruella's iconic colors are above all others black and white, seeing as half of her hair is black and the other white. Her beloved Dalmatian coat would of course also be black and white. Bright red is also a favorite color of hers.

What to Wear
Any type of fur or faux fur coat
Red, white or black gloves
Glamorous gowns
Graphic prints

Makeup
Cruella De Vil has thick black eyeliner and a brown or green eye shadow. Her lipstick is bright red and she often wears matching nail polish.

Accessories
Sunglasses
A chic purse
Glamorous jewelry
A plush Dalmatian
Green pendant earrings
Cigarette holder

Mother Gothel

What's the Story?
Mother Gothel is the charming and beautiful villain of *Tangled* where she poses as Rapunzel's mother figure! Gothel uses a magical flower that possesses the power of eternal youth. When the powers are transferred to baby Rapunzel's hair, Gothel kidnaps Rapunzel and locks her in a tower so only she can use the magical powers that keep her young forever! Mother Gothel cares only about herself and about staying young and beautiful. She is manipulative, elegant, sarcastic and clever.

Color Palette
Her dark curly hair is iconic and she usually wears a burgundy dress. Her palette is dark and eerie and deep dark red is the perfect fit!

What to Wear
A red dress with long sleeves
A long cape with a hood
Clothing with dark flower details
A belt around the hips and let the end of it hang loose down the length of the dress

Makeup
Wear mild makeup with brown colors and soft red lipstick

Accessories
Magic flower
A dagger
A hairbrush
A blond braid

What's the Story?

Lady Tremaine is Cinderella's evil stepmother. She abuses Cinderella and will do anything to marry her daughters off into a prestigious family to gain social status. She is a unique Disney villain since she possesses no magical powers and she exerts no physical force. She believes in maintaining her grace and keeping up appearances. Lady Tremaine is very cruel, selfish and controlling as well as being very graceful.

Color Palette

Lady Tremaine's usual colors are red, purple and blue along with her iconic grey hair with streaks of white in it.

What to Wear

An elegant dress with a big skirt
High colored shirt
A turtle neck button down shirt

Makeup

Lady Tremaine does not wear a lot of makeup. She wears minimal makeup that underlines her natural beauty. Mild colors and natural lipstick will do the trick.

Accessories

Green earring and a broach to match
Pumpkin
Glass slipper

Lady Tremaine

Queen of Hearts

What's the Story?

The Queen of Hearts is the sinister villain of the classic tale of *Alice in Wonderland*. She is tyrannical and often psychotic and is obsessed with beheading which she orders as a punishment for the smallest errors. She wishes for everyone to answer her with "Yes, your majesty" and her philosophy is that her way is the only way there is. She is very cruel, loud, explosive, pompous and irrational.

Color Palette

Her main colors are those of a deck of cards, white, black and red and her main icon is of course the heart shape. She is also often portrait with a yellow or golden crown.

What to Wear

A dress with a big skirt
Long or half sleeves
A coat with a high collar
Anything with a deck of cards

Makeup

She is often portrait with heavy blue eye shadow and red puckered or heart shaped lips. She also has distinctive black eyebrows.

Accessories

A deck of cards
A crown
A wand

Maleficent

Hairstyles

Braided Horns

1. Make a triangular parting for the bangs and take them aside.
2. Take medium sized locks of hairs from the top of the head in a ponytail high on the head above the ears.
3. Now take the bangs and make a Dutch braid all the way to the end. Let the braid lie down over the center parting.
4. Take a medium sized lock from one ponytail, divide it in three, and make a traditional braid all the way to the end. Repeat throughout the ponytail, until you have made three braids.

5. Do the same on the other side.
6. Now braid the three braids together in the same way as you make a traditional braid and fasten them at the end. Take the large braid and pull half of it through into a ponytail.
7. Note that you should not pull all the hair through the elastic.
8. Use the end of the big braid to conceal the elastics by wrapping it around the elastic on both sides.
9. Pull the horns into shape and fasten them securely with hairpins.

1

2

3

4

5

6

Braids of Power

1. Comb all the hair back to front over the forehead. Divide it in two parts with a center parting from the back of the head to the forehead. Start making a Dutch braid on one side of the head, working tightly from the back toward the forehead.
2. Braid all the way to the hairline at the side and continue to braid until the length of the hair is incorporated. Do the same on the other side.
3. Fold the end of the braid back alongside the braid, keeping some height at the front over the forehead to mimic the appearance of Maleficent's fierce horns. Pin the end down behind the braid to hide it.
4. Do the same on the other side. It works well to use long hairpins for the part of the braid you want to stick up to make the "horns" stiffer.
5. Pull the sides of the braid to enlarge the "horns" out to the sides.
6. Spray the hairdo with hairspray to secure it all in place.

Maleficent's Headband

1. Divide the hair on the top of the head in three parts one on the back of the head and two on each side, above the ears, but leave out the bangs.
2. Take the bangs aside.
3. Remove the clips from the hair but be careful not to lose the divisions. Take a fairly large lock on top of the head and backcomb it from the roots to the ends.
4. Place a hairband in front of the lock and start wrapping the hair around it.
5. Pin the ends down underneath the hairband until it is steady.
6. Next take fairly large locks and backcomb them from the roots to the ends around the hairband area. Wrap each lock around the hairband and fasten it down with small hairpins. Repeat this until the hairband has disappeared underneath hair.
7. Make delicate partings for the bangs and bring the hair, alternately crossing from left to right and vice versa to form a zigzag parting. Pin the ends down with small hairpins.
8. Wrap the hair thoroughly up over the hairband.
9. Bring the hair from the sides tightly along the head behind the horns, and pin it down in the middle of the head at the back quite high up. Take the loose hair from the back and curl it all the way to the ends. Spray over with hairspray and comb lightly with a coarse hairbrush.

The Queen of Horns

1. Divide the hair on the top of the head in three parts one on the back of the head and two on each side, above the ears, but leave out the bangs.
2. Take a fairly large lock on the top of the head, and backcomb it from the roots the ends.
3. Place a hairband in front of the lock and start wrapping hair around it. Pin the end down underneath the hairband.
4. Next take fairly large locks and backcomb them from the roots to the ends around the hairband area. Wrap each lock around the hairband and fasten it down with small hairpins. Repeat this until the hairband has disappeared underneath the hair and horns have formed.
5. Bring the hair from the sides tightly along the head behind the horns, and pin it down in the middle at the back quite high up. Take the loose hair at the back and roll it tightly up towards the nape of the neck.
6. Include the rest of the hair ends, and wrap them together with the hair from higher up the back of the head. Fasten with hairpins.
7. It works best to fasten the hairpins by hooking them in the twist and pressing them down against the twist, that way they hold tightly.
8. Spray over with hairspray.

Evil Queen

Hairstyles

Magic Mirror Side Braid

1. Start by combing the hair completely to one side.
2. Next divide it unevenly and backcomb the roots to produce a lot of lift and volume on top of the head.
3. Comb lightly over the top layer of the hair to hide the backcombing.
4. Make a traditional braid with the hair.
5. Make the braid lie nicely down one side of the head.
6. Secure the end of the braid with an elastic band and spray the hair with hairspray.

Royal Curls

1. Comb the hair thoroughly and spray with hairspray to help the style hold.
2. Start by dividing the hair in two sections horizontally from ear to ear, across the back of the head.
3. Curl the lower section starting at the sides and going around the back of the head.

4. Repeat this process on the top section and then backcomb the roots slightly on top of the head and spray over with hairspray. Place a few locks on top of the head to lend greater height to the hairdo.

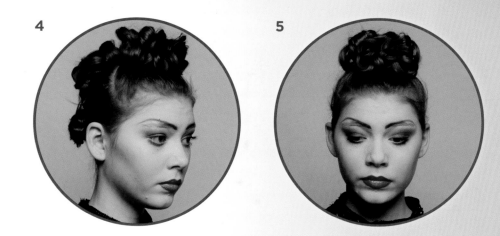

A Curly Crown

1. Start by dividing the hair in three sections horizontally across the back of the head, and put the sections in elastic bands to make ponytails.
2. Make each ponytail wavy, using a medium gauge curling iron. Place each lock on top of the head around its ponytail.
3. Pin the locks randomly atop the head until they form a mohawk.
4. Position the locks so that all the elastics are well concealed.
5. Make one or two loose knots in each of the locks on the top of the head. Place them systematically around the elastic until a kind of a "crown" has been formed.

1

2

3

4

5

6

7

8

9

A Braided Tiara

1. Comb the hair forward from the crown of the head to make it easier to neatly incorporate locks into a braid.
2. Start making a Dutch braid by one ear.
3. Continue along the hairline, taking care to make the partings neat from the crown of the head, so that it is easier to follow the hairline.
4. When all the hair has been added to the Dutch braid, continue with a normal braid down the length of the hair.
5. Once the braid has been made all the way to the end, go back to the beginning of the braid and gently pull its sides. It is important to spend time on this part, the more you pull at its side, the bigger and more majestic the braid becomes.
6. Now take the end of the braid and roll it up to the head.
7. Coil the end in under the braid to conceal it.
8. Pin the end by hooking a pin in the ends of the braid and fastening it under the braid in the hair at the nape of the neck.
9. Pull the braid at the top of the head upwards to increase its height and to form a tiara.

Ursula

Hairstyles

White and Wavy

1. Comb the hair thoroughly.
2. Divide the hair across the head, from ear to ear, creating front and back sections of hair.
3. Take the front section, around the forehead, and backcomb it all, from the roots to the ends.
4. Comb lightly over it to make a smoother appearance, then wrap the end around your finger and roll it down towards the head, making sure you keep good height on top of the head.
5. Pin it down behind the roll so the pins are hidden.
6. On the back section of hair, use a medium gauge curling iron to add waves throughout the entire section, from roots to tips.
7. Spray hairspray all over the hair to maintain the look. Spraying the bangs with white hairspray will help you achieve this fun Ursula look.

Streaming Curls

1. Divide the hair in three sections; one large section of bangs across the front of the head and two sections on the back of the head by parting the remaining hair down the center. Secure the two back sections into medium-high pigtails.
2. Conceal the elastics by taking a small lock from each pigtail and wrapping it around the elastic. Take fairly large locks from the pigtails and curl them separately.
3. Do this for both the pigtails and spray over with hairspray.
4. Next, work on the bangs section, backcombing it from the roots to the ends. Gather the ends together and roll them down to the head.
5. Take care to keep a good volume in the bangs. It works well to stick a pintail comb a little into the bangs to comb under and up against the bangs.
6. Pin the lock behind the bangs.
7. Next take the curled locks in the pigtails, and pin them onto the head.
8. Let a few locks hang over the face. Finish pinning all the locks up onto the head, and spray the hairdo with hairspray. It is fun to spray the bangs with white hairspray, too.

1

2

3

4

5

6

7

8

9

Ocean of Braids & Curls

1. Start by combing all the hair forward, then divide the hair horizontally across the top of the head, from ear to ear, and clip the front section away.
2. On the back section, make a Dutch braid, from the nape of the neck upward toward the crown.
3. Fasten the Dutch braid with an elastic band, up against the head.
4. Continue braiding the length of the hair and fasten with another small elastic at the end of the braid, and place the length of the braid on top of the Dutch braid. Note that if the hair is not very long, it is possible to

let the end of the Dutch braid connect with the bangs area.
5. Pin the end down to the head at the nape of the neck.
6. Fasten with a few hairpins all the way up the braid.
7. Take hold of the front section of the hair, creating a ponytail at the top of the head. Curl the ends with a medium gauge curling iron.
8. Pin the locks down alongside the elastic and let them hang over the face.
9. Pull the locks in the top area out to the sides. Spray over with hairspray.

Larger than Life

1. Start by spraying the hair with hairspray to increase its volume. Then curl the entire head of hair with a medium gauge curling iron.
2. Separate out big locks and backcomb them from the roots to the ends until they are very stiff. It works well to backcomb a few backcombed locks together again and again.
3. Take the locks and spray them with hairspray. Pin the locks to the head, until they become tight and stick lightly out into the air.
4. Continue placing the locks, until they stick out on their own accord. Then spray over with strong hold hairspray.
5. Spray a random selection of locks with white hairspray to finish the look.

Note: When combing through the hair after backcombing, it is important that the hair is dry, and to start at the ends and work towards the roots.

Captain Hook

Hairstyles

1

2

3

4

5

6

Braided Dreads

1. Make a horseshoe parting in the hair around the crown of the head and clip the upper section away.
2. Separate small locks out from the hair left hanging and make braids, starting on one side and working toward the back of the head.
3. Braid each lock all the way down and put an elastic band at the end.
4. Do the same on the other side of the head, working toward the back.
5. Loosen the top section and braid it in the same way.
6. Let the braids hang freely. Pull gently on the sides of each braid to make it thicker. If you would like, it is possible to backcomb the ends of the braids to secure them without using elastic bands

1

2

3

4

5

6

7

Crazy Curls

1. Comb through the hair and separate the top hair from the hair around the sides and back of the head.
2. Clip the top section away and curl the loose hair in small sections, starting by the ears and moving toward the back of the head.
3. When the locks are small, the curls will be better defined.
4. Continue until all the hair has been curled. Be sure to make a center part before the last locks on top of the head are curled.
5. Comb through the hair with your fingers.
6. Divide and pull apart the locks to achieve a coarser texture for the curls.
7. Take some locks here and there and pin them to the top of the head. Let a few locks fall over the forehead. Spray the entire head of hair with hairspray.

1

2

3

4

The Captain

1. Add waves throughout the hair with a large gauge curling iron, and spray hairspray all over the head.
2. Loosen the waves by combing the hair thoroughly.
3. Make a side parting, take the hair at the back of the head and pin it up.

4. Join the locks together at either side and let them lie over the shoulders.

Note: It is possible to decorate with a large feather or to wear a fun hat with this hairdo.

Pirate Parrot

1. Divide the hair in four sections horizontally on the head, from front to back.
2. Put an elastic band around each part.
3. Arrange the elastics so that they form a diagonal line from the front to the back of the head.
4. Next use a curling iron to curl the front ponytail in small pieces so that it has many small curls.
5. Repeat this for each ponytail separately.
6. When all the locks have been curled from the four ponytails, pin each lock separately up near the elastic.
7. Repeat this process for each ponytail.
8. Shape the hairdo so that a diagonal line forms from one side at the front to the other side at the back. Adjust the locks slightly, to make the mohawk fuller.

Cruella de Vil

Hairstyles

Glamorous Buns

1. Divide the hair in two with a center parting.
2. Put each part in a ponytail and secure them with elastic bands.
3. Place one of the ponytails directly above the ear, and the other higher up on the head.
4. Backcomb medium sized locks from both ponytails all the way to the ends. Take care to backcomb all the hair.
5. Place a hair donut around one of the ponytails, and fasten it with 2-3 hairpins. Create the other bun with the hair from the ponytail.
6. Make the second bun a different shape than the other.
7. Adjust the hair a little in each bun to enlarge them, and pin them down.
8. Take care to make the buns different. It is fun to spray the hair on one side with white hair spray just like Cruella de Vil.

Fashionista Waves

1. Comb your hair thoroughly and part it down the center. Use a medium gauge curling iron to add waves to one side of the head, starting at the front and working toward the back. Keep the curling iron 2 inches away from the scalp, but curl all the way to the end of each strand.
2. Repeat this process on the other side of your head.
3. When all the hair has become wavy, spray it with hairspray.
4. Before combing through the locks, let the hairspray dry a little. This will add more texture to the hair. Comb all the locks on each side well together.

Note: You'll really look like Cruella if you spray one side of your hair with white hairspray.

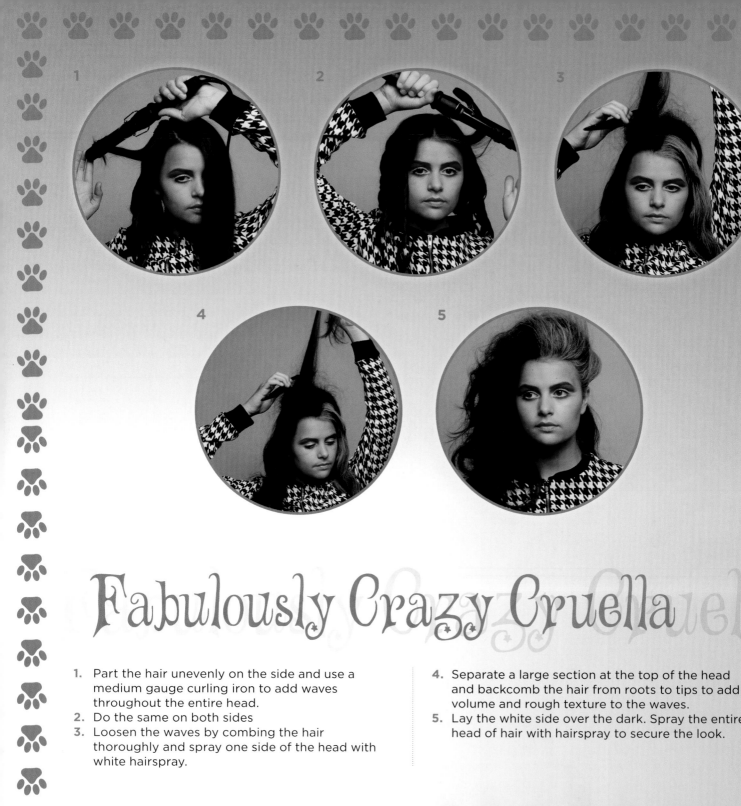

Fabulously Crazy Cruella

1. Part the hair unevenly on the side and use a medium gauge curling iron to add waves throughout the entire head.
2. Do the same on both sides
3. Loosen the waves by combing the hair thoroughly and spray one side of the head with white hairspray.
4. Separate a large section at the top of the head and backcomb the hair from roots to tips to add volume and rough texture to the waves.
5. Lay the white side over the dark. Spray the entire head of hair with hairspray to secure the look.

Mother Gothel

Hairstyles

Braided Tangle

1. Comb the hair well and divide it in two with a center parting. Pin away the hair from one half of the head.
2. On the side of the head with loose hair, make two more partings to divide the hair in three sections. Braid each section and secure it with an elastic band. You'll have three braids on the side of your head.
3. Do the same thing on the other side with the hair you had previously pinned away.
4. Gently pull the sides of the braids to make them larger. Do this with all the braids.
5. Braid all three braids on one side of the head together in one large traditional braid. Take out the small elastics when you reach the end of the large braid, and secure the new braid with one larger elastic band. Finally, pull the large braid a little to give it more volume and texture.
6. Do the same on the other side.
7. Spread both braids widely by pulling their sides.

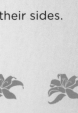

A Tower of Hair

1. Start by dividing the hair in two sections, horizontally across the back of the head. Then take the top section and divide it in three smaller sections horizontally on the head. Pin them aside for now.
2. Use a medium gauge curling iron to create waves in the back section of the hair, keeping the iron 2 inches away from the scalp and curling through to the ends of each strand.
3. Of the three sections of hair pinned aside, backcomb the section closest to the face.
4. Comb lightly through the lock for a nice texture. Take hold of the end and wrap it around your finger and keep rolling it from the face towards the back of the head. Pin the end down behind the lock.
5. Repeat this in the next section. Note that it is important to keep a lot of height and body over the whole head.
6. Hide the hairpin inside the lock.
7. The third and last lock is rolled down forward and fastened. Finally you should spray over with hairspray.
8. Keep the locks tight together and pull the hair as needed for maximum height.

Magical Curls

1. Comb the hair and part it down the middle, dividing it into two sections.
2. Concentrate on one side at a time, and start by curling each lock separately from the roots to the ends.
3. Continue this method until all the hair has been curled.
4. Now take a large lock on top of the head, and backcomb the roots thoroughly.
5. You may need to go back over the locks on top of your head with the curling iron, as they can become frizzy from the backcombing.
6. Pull the curls slightly to loosen them and spray the style with hairspray.

Madam Mim

Hairstyles

4
5

Batty Bangs

1. Comb your hair thoroughly, so it easier to put in a ponytail.
2. Place the ponytail at the top of the head, securing it with an elastic band.
3. Put another elastic around the same ponytail, but only pull half the hair through it, making sure that the ends are placed on top of the head towards the forehead. To hide the elastic, it is possible to take a small lock from the ponytail and wrap it around the elastic band.

4. Backcomb all the bangs, spray them with hairspray to make them stiffer, then backcomb them again.
5. Spread the backcombed ends well over the forehead and back over the sides of the head.

To really look like Madam Mim you can spray your hair with purple hairspray.

Wacky Violet

1. Pull the hair in a high ponytail, securing it with an elastic band and backcomb the ponytail.
2. Once the whole ponytail has been back-combed lay strands of it along the head all the way around.
3. Pin the strands of hair tightly to the head so that it looks unkempt from forehead to the back of the head.

4. Spray all over the hair with medium hold hair-spray.

Note: It is fun to finish off the hairdo by spraying it with purple hairspray.

Spellbound

1. Comb through the hair and make a center parting.
2. Take a large lock of hair on one side and backcomb it from the roots to the ends. Repeat on the other side.
3. Comb lightly through the hair, taking care to keep the hairdo very airy on the top of the head on each side.
4. Gather the hair on each side by the ends and secure the gathered pieces with an elastic band. It is fun to spray the hair lightly with purple hairspray to get Madam Mim's look.

Magical Messy Braid

1. Make a deep side part in the hair.
2. Comb the hair to the side.
3. Make a fishtail braid in the hair by splitting the large section of hair in two and taking a small lock from the furthest right, bringing it over the right section, and then under the left section. Join the lock with the left section.

4. Take another small lock from the furthest left section and bring it over toward and under the right section. Join the lock to the right section. Repeat this process down the length of the hair.
5. Put an elastic band at the end to secure the fishtail braid. Spray your hair with purple hairspray to finish the look.

Lady Tremaine

Hairstyles

A Posh Spiral

1. Comb the hair completely straight before you start, make a large parting separating the bangs and clip them away.
2. Backcomb all the roots to make the hairdo fuller, aiming to get the biggest lift at the top of the head.
3. The hair needs a lot of body, so thorough backcombing is in order.
4. Comb lightly through the top layer of the hair all the way down to achieve a sleek surface. Then start twisting the hair away from the face, from the cheek to the back of the head.
5. Do the same on the other side; twist the hair away from the face, from the cheek to the back of the head. Join the spirals in a ponytail with an elastic band at the back of the head. Take a lock from the ponytail, and wrap it around the elastic to hide it.
6. Next divide the bangs and backcomb the roots lightly.
7. Comb the lock lightly together, and wrap it in a circle around your finger, rolling it all the way down to the head. Open the lock slightly to make it look majestic and choose where to fasten it.
8. Pin the lock at the back, hiding the hairpin inside the bangs. To really look like Lady Tremaine spray the sides and the bangs with white hairspray creating streaks.

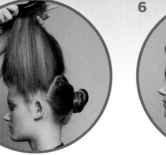

Regal Bun

1. Divide the hair in two, horizontally across the back of the head. Separate out one small piece of hair from each side of the head and leave them loose. Backcomb all the hair at the roots in the top section except for the small pieces you've separated.

2. Gather the lower section together and comb the hair thoroughly. Take a firm hold of the section up by the head and twist it.

3. Continue twisting the lower section until it has been twisted into a bun tight to the head.

4. Try and make the twist as even as you can all the way around. Fasten the bun with hairpins.

5. Take the top section, which you backcombed, and comb lightly through the outer hairs to make the section appear smoother. Hold the end and wrap the section around your finger, then roll it down to the head, and fasten it with a hairpin.

6. Take the pieces of hair left loose on either side of your head and place them over the backcombed area pinning them down behind the backcombed section.

7. Try and make the upper section of the hair look as smooth as possible to hide the backcombing.

8. Spray white hairspray in the sides and at the top to achieve the wicked look of Lady Tremaine.

Properly Proper Curls

1. Divide the hair in two, horizontally across the back of the head. Separate out one small piece of hair from each side of the head and leave them loose. Backcomb all the hair at the roots in the top section except for the small pieces you've separated.
2. Take hold of the top section and comb lightly through the outer hairs to make the section appear smoother. Hold the end of the section and wrap it around your finger and then roll it down to the head, and fasten it with a hairpin.
3. Take the hair left loose by the hairline and place it over the backcombed area, pinning it down behind the backcombed section. Spray the sides and the top with white hairspray.
4. Try to keep this top section looking smooth and even, hiding the backcombing.
5. Now divide the back section of hair into large parts and curl with a medium gauge curling iron.
6. Curl each lock separately, approximately 1 inch from the roots to the ends.
7. Repeat throughout the lower section.
8. Spray the entire head of hair with hairspray.

Queen of Hearts

Hairstyles

A Wand of Power

1. Comb the hair thoroughly.
2. Put a high ponytail in the hair, placed slightly to one side, and secure it in place with an elastic band.
3. Take another elastic and put it around the pony-tail, but only pull half the length of the hair through. Make the ends of the ponytail fall over the forehead. Finally you put two extra elastics around the hair that went through the second elastic.
4. Pin the ends of the ponytail down on top of the head.
5. Backcomb the ends lightly and spray them with hairspray.
6. Make the ends of the bangs stick up into the air a little and accessorize with a small tiara.

Off With Their Heads!

1. Comb all your hair to the side.
2. Start making a Dutch braid by one ear, bringing it up along the hairline by the forehead.
3. Continue until you reach the back of the head.
4. Braid the length of your hair and fasten the braid with an elastic band.

5. You can hide the elastic band by wrapping a small strand of hair from the end of the braid around it and securing it in place with a hairpin.
6. Finish the look with a small tiara on top of the head.

Crown of Hearts

1. Start by dividing the hair into top and bottom sections, and clip the top section away.
2. Use a medium gauge curling iron to make waves throughout the bottom section, curling medium sized strands at a time and staying 2 inches away from the scalp.
3. Repeat this throughout the back of the head. Spray the waves with hairspray.
4. Divide the top section in two horizontally.
5. Backcomb the section further from the face, from the roots to the ends.
6. Take the backcombed part and roll it down to the head, making a kind of a round filling.
7. Next, take delicate partings from the front section and place them over the "round filling". Fasten them with little hairpins and repeat this until all the hair has been laid over the filling.
8. Place a pretty band or a decoration around the filling and fasten it at the back underneath the ends of the front section. Take the ends and curl them lightly.
9. Fix the height and take care to make it even and pretty. Spray over with hairspray.

1

2

3

4

5

Around and Around

1. Start by dividing the hair in two sections, horizontally from ear to ear. Make the lower part wavy using medium gauge curling iron. Divide the top section in two with a center part. Backcomb both parts from the roots to the ends.
2. Take one of the top parts and roll it towards the head, leaving a good space at the top of the head.
3. Do the same on the other side, taking care to make the rolls on both sides even. Pin the back section of the rolls together, so no gap forms between them.
4. Pin the hair securely. A good number of hairpins may be required, as the hair tends to be rather heavy when it lies at the brim of the head.
5. Place a crown in the middle of the top section to finish the look.

Index